Hello, Family Members,

Learning to read is one of the most important accomplishments of early childhood. **Hello Reader!** books are designed to help children become skilled readers who like to read. Beginning readers learn to read by remembering frequently used words like "the," "is," and "and"; by using phonics skills to decode new words; and by interpreting picture and text clues. These books provide both the stories children enjoy and the structure they need to read fluently and independently. Here are suggestions for helping your child *before*, *during*, and *after* reading:

Before

- Look at the cover and pictures and have your child predict what the story is about.
- Read the story to your child.
- Encourage your child to chime in with familiar words and phrases.
- Echo read with your child by reading a line first and having your child read it after you do.

During

- Have your child think about a word he or she does not recognize right away. Provide hints such as "Let's see if we know the sounds" and "Have we read other words like this one?"
- Encourage your child to use phonics skills to sound out new words.
- Provide the word for your child when more assistance is needed so that he or she does not struggle and the experience of reading with you is a positive one.
- Encourage your child to have fun by reading with a lot of expression . . . like an actor!

After

- Have your child keep lists of interesting and favorite words.
- Encourage your child to read the books over and over again. Have him or her read to brothers, sisters, grandparents, and even teddy bears. Repeated readings develop confidence in young readers.
- Talk about the stories. Ask and answer questions. Share ideas about the funniest and most interesting characters and events in the stories.

I do hope that you and your child enjoy this book.

> —Francie Alexander
> Chief Education Officer,
> Scholastic's Learning Ventures

To the California kids:
Chris, Sylvia, Teresa, Chris, Jr.,
and Michelle
—L.J.H.

To California earthquake survivor
Bruce Glasberg
—J.W.

ISBN 0-439-20545-X

Text copyright © 2002 by Lorraine Jean Hopping.
Illustrations copyright © 2002 by Jody Wheeler.
All rights reserved. Published by Scholastic Inc.
SCHOLASTIC, HELLO READER, CARTWHEEL BOOKS, and associated
logos are trademarks and/or registered trademarks of Scholastic Inc.

Library of Congress Cataloging-in-Publication Data
Hopping, Lorraine Jean.
 Wild earth : earthquake! / by Lorraine Jean Hopping ; illustrated by Jody Wheeler.
  p.   cm.—(Hello reader! Level 4)
 ISBN 0-439-20545-X (pbk.)
1. Earthquakes—Juvenile literature. [1. Earthquakes.] I. Wheeler, Jody, ill. II. Title.
III. Series

12 11 10 9 8 7 6 5 4 3 2 1   02 03 04 05 06

Printed in the U.S.A.   24
First printing, April 2002

Earthquake!

by Lorraine Jean Hopping
Illustrated by Jody Wheeler

Hello Reader! Science — Level 4

SCHOLASTIC INC.

Cartwheel
·B·O·O·K·S·®

New York   Toronto   London   Auckland   Sydney
Mexico City   New Delhi   Hong Kong   Buenos Aires

Chapter 1

The Pancaked Building

Evan Lewis guessed that the building once stood six or eight stories high. It was hard to tell exactly.

Now, all the floors and ceilings were smashed together.

The concrete slabs stood one on top of another like a stack of pancakes.

It was a surprisingly short stack. The former apartment building was now just a little taller than Evan.

Evan was part of a special rescue team from the United States.

The team was in Izmit, Turkey. A terrible earthquake had just killed thousands of people in that city. Rescuers were working nonstop to save as many lives as they could.

The earthquake had struck on August 17, 1999, at 3:02 A.M.

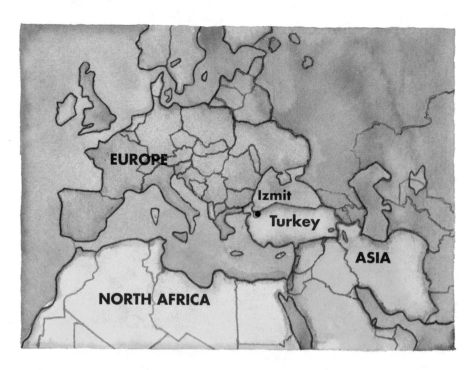

Eight-year-old Mehmet Yazci
[yahz-jeh] was asleep when it hit.
His bedroom was near the top
of an apartment building in Izmit.
For 45 seconds, the boy's body shook
so hard that it hurt.
His bed and belongings jumped
around like popping corn.

The walls cracked and crumbled.
Then—*BOOM!*—the ceiling fell.

Somehow, the ceiling stopped just short of crushing Mehmet. Something held it in place just above his body.

Mehmet was trapped in a dark space the size of a car trunk. Scared but unhurt, he lay quietly in his blue pajamas.

The next day, a rescue team looked
and listened for signs of life in the
pancaked building.
Search dogs sniffed for a human scent.
But Mehmet was buried too deeply
inside the fallen building.

Finding no signs of life, the team
quickly moved on.
They had a city of rubble to search.
And the hours were passing fast.

To Mehmet, time passed far too slowly.
Two days came and went.
With no food or water, the boy
grew weak.

On the third day, Mehmet heard
a digging machine above him.
He yelled as loud as he could.

A voice yelled back!
The digging machine stopped.

"A boy!" someone shouted in Turkish.
"A boy is alive!"

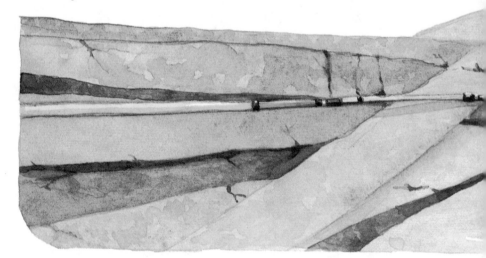

Rescue teams rushed to the scene.
They put a search camera inside
the pancaked building.
The end of the long pole had a
camera, speaker, and microphone.

The TV camera showed rescuers
exactly where the boy was.
The speaker let Mehmet's uncle talk
to his nephew.

"I'm okay," the boy told him.

Evan Lewis and his squad set up a hammer and drill machine.
The loud machine cut a hole in the concrete above Mehmet's head.

Evan was the smallest rescuer, and so he crawled down the tiny hole.
About four feet down, he felt the boy's soft body.
Evan gave Mehmet a face mask to protect him from clouds of dust.

"Protecting the patient is the one thing you always have on your mind," Evan said later.

Evan cut away the rails around Mehmet's bed and sawed off part of the wood frame.
Finally, he was able to lift the boy into the hands of another rescuer.

Mehmet Yazci lost his parents and
two sisters in the earthquake.
But he was alive and unhurt.

Chapter 2

A Whole Lot of Shaking

Earthquakes are sudden movements of the ground that make it shake. The more ground that moves, the bigger the quake.
The bigger the quake, the longer the shake.

The biggest quake in modern times shook for at least four minutes. That's twice as long as a roller coaster ride.

The quake hit just off the coast of Chile, South America, in 1960. The sudden movement of the ocean floor kicked up a **tsunami** [soo-NAH-mee] wave.

The huge wave zoomed across the Pacific Ocean as fast as an airplane. It flooded cities in places as far away as Hawaii and Japan.

Hilo, Hawaii, 1960

The second biggest quake struck
Alaska four years later, in 1964.
It also lasted more than four minutes
and created a tsunami.

During those terrible minutes,
thousands of miles of earth moved.
In Prince William Sound, part of the
seafloor rose out of the water.
It was lifted an amazing ten meters,
or about 30 feet.
That's equal to a three-story building!

Prince William Sound, Alaska, 1964

Somewhere, the ground is moving
and shaking right now.
That's because thousands of
earthquakes happen every day.
Only about a hundred of them are
big enough for people to feel.

former seafloor

The size of an earthquake is called its **magnitude** [MAG-nih-tood].

The weakest earthquakes, magnitude 1 or 2, are very minor. People can't feel very minor quakes.

People can barely feel minor quakes, the next biggest quakes on the chart.

Moderate and strong quakes can cause some damage.
They happen somewhere in the world about once or twice a day on average.

Major quakes, like the one in Turkey, can cause serious damage. They strike about once or twice a month on average.

Earthquake Magnitudes

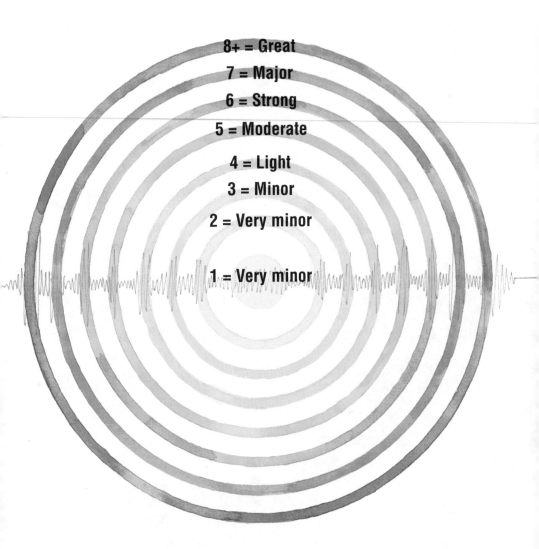

8+ = Great
7 = Major
6 = Strong
5 = Moderate
4 = Light
3 = Minor
2 = Very minor
1 = Very minor

Magni- means "strong." Strong quakes have higher magnitudes than weak ones.

In 1989, a major quake struck near
San Francisco, California.
The quake was named Loma Prieta
[pree-AY-tah], after a mountain.
The name means "very black hill."

Baseball players were warming up
for a World Series game when the
shaking began.
The game was never played.
The whole World Series was called
off due to earthquake damage in and
around San Francisco.

The top deck of a double-decker
highway fell onto the bottom deck,
crushing dozens of cars and people.

Town houses were tossed around
like building blocks.
They were built on soft soil.
Many of them sank partway into
the ground.

In 1999, a major quake in Taiwan [tye-WAN], Asia, tipped over a very tall skyscraper.
The quake's strong jolts caused a rice factory to explode.

In 2001, a major quake flattened many towns in the nation of India.
Tens of thousands of Indians lost their lives.
Half a million lost their homes.

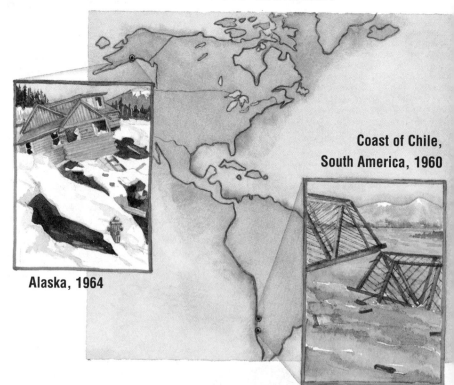

Coast of Chile, South America, 1960

Alaska, 1964

Major quakes are damaging and
deadly.
Yet they're not the biggest quakes.
Great quakes, like those in Chile
and Alaska, are many times bigger
than major quakes.
They strike about once a year on
average.

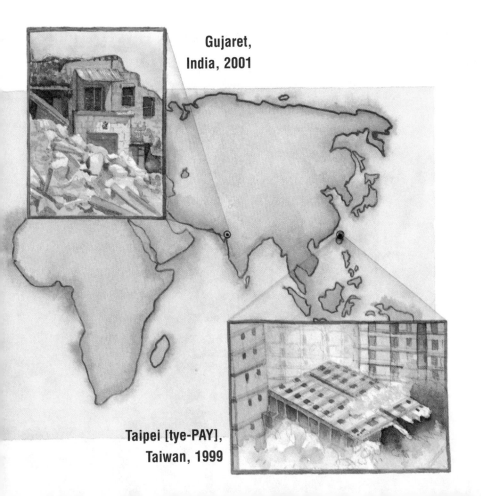

Gujaret,
India, 2001

Taipei [tye-PAY],
Taiwan, 1999

A famous great quake jolted
San Francisco in 1906.

Farmers said that flat ground moved
like ocean waves.
The "land waves" rippled up and
down across their fields.

A road split in two.
The two halves moved 15 feet apart.

Sailors at sea thought their boats
had slammed into rocks.
Instead, shocks from the quake had
jolted their floating boats.

In downtown San Francisco,
buildings crumbled.
When chimneys fell, fires spread.
More than 50 fires burned for three
days, destroying most of the city.

San Francisco,
California, 1906

Chapter 3

Finding Faults

Could a big quake hit your area?
This map shows where big quakes
are common in the United States.
Darker colors show places where there
is a great danger of earthquakes.

Alaska and California are two
well-known earthquake states.
But look at the small dark spot
labeled "New Madrid."
In December 1811, two major quakes
jolted New Madrid, Missouri.
Then, in February 1812, an even bigger
quake struck the same area.

People in Charleston, South Carolina,
felt the shaking. Charleston is 600
miles from New Madrid!

Earthquake Danger in the United States

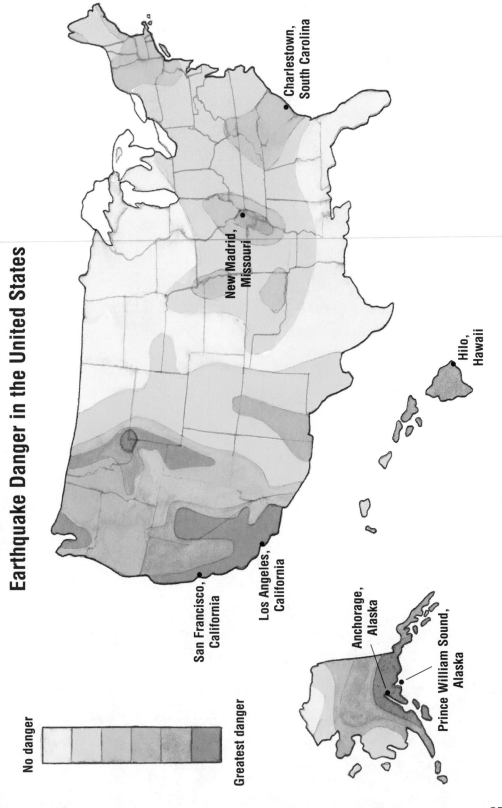

No danger

Greatest danger

Charlestown, South Carolina

New Madrid, Missouri

Hilo, Hawaii

San Francisco, California

Los Angeles, California

Anchorage, Alaska

Prince William Sound, Alaska

Tom Holzer, an earthquake scientist, locates places where quakes might strike in the future.

One way is to look for places where the earth has moved in the past. For example, Tom searches for lines of broken ground called **faults**.

The ground on one side of a fault moves very slowly one way. The ground on the other side creeps the opposite way.

Think of your knuckles as a fault.
Press them together as shown below.
Try to move one fist up and the other
fist down.
Your knuckles get in the way.
But if you move your fists hard
enough, they jerk past each other.

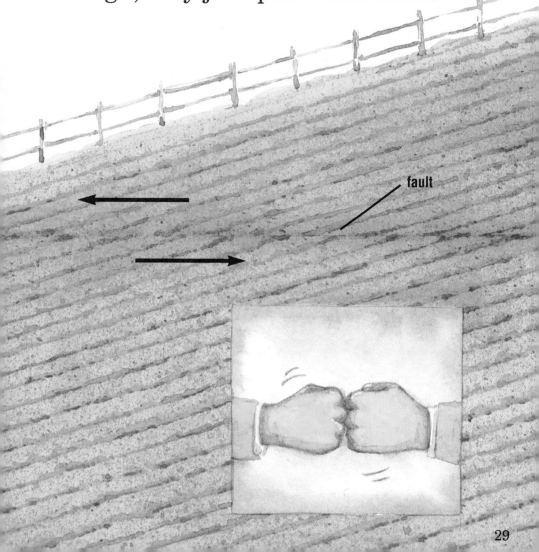

fault

An earthquake happens when two sides of a fault jerk past each other. After the sudden slip, the two sides get stuck again and stop.

Sometimes, one side slides up while the other slides down. Up-and-down movement is called a **dip-slip fault**.

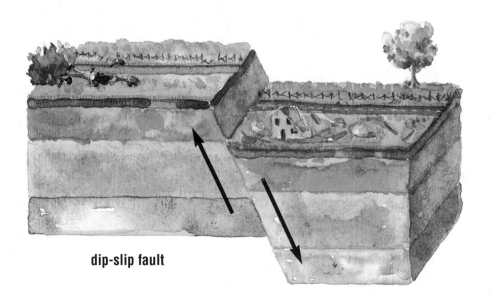

dip-slip fault

The two chunks of ground can also slide side-by-side.
This is called a **strike-slip fault**.

Tom Holzer lives near a famous strike-slip fault.
The San Andreas [an-DRAY-uhs] fault runs the length of California and beyond. (See page 41.)
Countless smaller faults lie near the San Andreas.

strike-slip fault

Earthquake scientists make maps
of faults, big and small.
Fault maps help people avoid
building directly on a fault line.

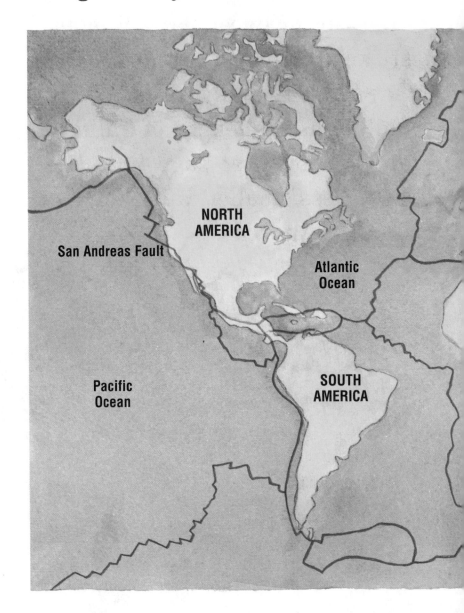

The maps also show which towns
are close to dangerous faults.
This map shows the world's big
earthquake faults.

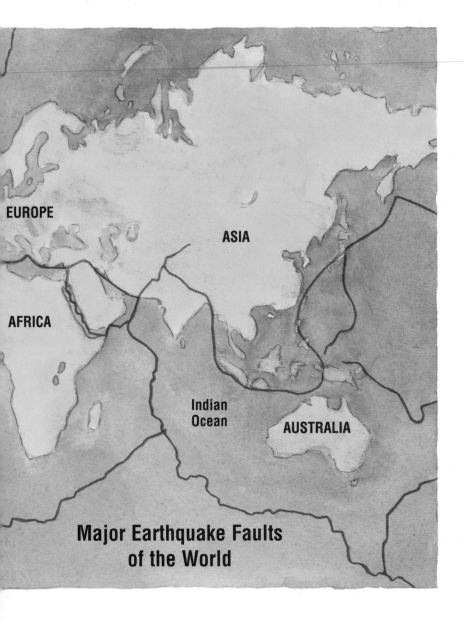

EUROPE

ASIA

AFRICA

Indian
Ocean

AUSTRALIA

**Major Earthquake Faults
of the World**

People in those towns can make
their buildings stronger.
For example, they can build with
extra-strong concrete and steel.
They can also add cross-braces
to the walls.
With braces, a building can shake
harder without falling down.

What happens to buildings that are
not strong?
In Turkey, the pancaked building
was made of cheap materials.

"It was easy to cut a hole through
the concrete," Evan Lewis said.

Many other buildings that fell had
weak concrete, too.

Cutaway of a House

cross-brace

Chapter 4

For Sure!

Tom Holzer was in the Loma Prieta
earthquake of 1989.
He admits it was scary.

"It's like standing up in a shaky
canoe," Tom said.

Yet Tom does something far more
dangerous than live near faults.
He rides a bike to work each day!

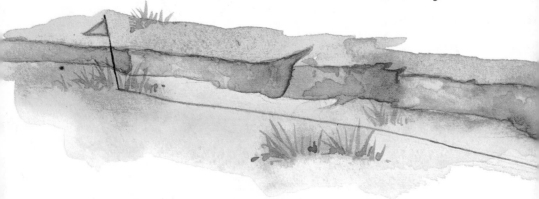

People are far more likely to die in a traffic accident than in an earthquake. In fact, lightning kills more people than earthquakes do.

Like Tom, Lucy Jones lives and works near earthquake faults. She is the chief earthquake scientist in southern California.

Lucy says the fear of earthquakes is much greater than the risk. One reason is that earthquakes are impossible to predict. They strike with no warning.

"You can see a storm coming," Lucy said. "You know it will rain."

There is no way to know when a big earthquake is about to strike.

"We'll have 30 or 40 earthquakes
in Los Angeles today," Lucy said.
"And a big earthquake starts out
exactly like a small one. The ground
starts to shake."

Machines called **seismographs**
[SIZE-muh-grafs] record the shaking
as zigs and zags.
The shaking usually stops in a few
seconds.
But some day, it will keep going.
And going.

Some day, for sure, a great
earthquake will strike California.
Scientists can't say what day, what
year, or even what decade.
But great quakes have hit California
before, and so one will hit again.

California won't fall into the sea.
The earth won't open up and swallow
people.
But a great quake will cause serious
damage and loss of life.

Lucy's science team will be ready.
The scientists will collect data on
the magnitude of the earthquake.
The magnitude gives them an idea
of the amount of damage.

They will map its **epicenter**
[EP-ih-SEN-ter].
The epicenter is an imaginary spot
on the surface of the ground.
Below it, under the ground, is the
place where the earth started to
move, causing the quake.
The shaking is hardest near the
epicenter.

City officials will use the map to help people.
For example, they can send rescue teams to areas near the epicenter.

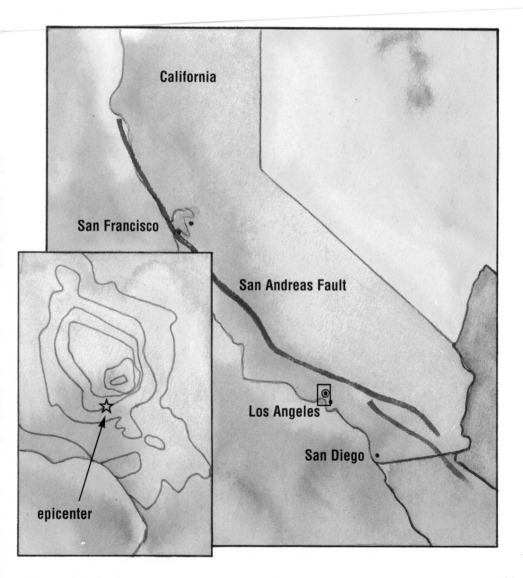

California

San Francisco

San Andreas Fault

Los Angeles

San Diego

epicenter

Chapter 5

Fighting the Fear

In 1994, a very strong earthquake
struck near Los Angeles, California.
Lucy Jones was happy to be there.
She wanted to study the quake.
But most people were scared.
They wanted to be anyplace else.

The earthquake tore down a raised
highway.
It toppled buildings and homes.

Soon after the quake, Lucy spoke
to a fourth-grade class.
The students were terrified.

Lucy told them how to protect
themselves in an earthquake.
(See "Safety Tips," page 48.)
She said to keep a pair of shoes
under their beds at all times.
Earthquakes break things,
especially glass.
Shoes help people walk out of
damaged houses.

Lucy also told the class to get set for **aftershocks**, earthquakes that strike in the days after a main quake. Aftershocks are usually smaller than the main quake.
Lucy taught the students how to measure magnitude.

"Bigger earthquakes shake longer," Lucy said. "So just count the total seconds of shaking."

To count seconds, you can say, "One California, two California, three California," and so on.
Each "California" takes a second.

Next, Lucy told how to estimate the distance to the epicenter.

Quakes cause two types of shaking. First, people feel light shaking called **P waves**.
The shaking might feel like a rumbling truck is passing nearby. Then people feel much harder shaking from **S waves**.

Lucy told the students to count the seconds between the start of the P waves and the start of the S waves. The more seconds they count, the farther away the epicenter is.

For example, five seconds means the epicenter is about a mile away.
Ten seconds means it is about two miles away.

After Lucy's talk, the fourth graders didn't feel as scared.
Now, they had a job to do!

The next time students felt an earthquake, they took cover at once.
Instead of feeling helpless, they made observations.
They fought their fear with science.

Earthquake Safety Tips

If you feel the ground shake, follow these tips right away:

- If you are outside, move away from buildings or other objects and drop to the ground.
- If you are inside, move to the center of the room, if you can.
- Drop to the floor and hide under a big table or desk.
- Hold onto the table or desk until the shaking stops.
- After the shaking stops, go outside. Do not go back inside until an official tells you it's safe.
- Stay away from power lines and damaged buildings.